HISTORY THROUGH
NeWspApErs

THE
CUBAN
MISSILE CRISIS

Nathaniel Harris

HODDER
Wayland

an imprint of Hodder Children's Books

Produced for Hodder Wayland by
Discovery Books Ltd
Unit 3, 37 Watling Street, Leintwardine, Shropshire SY7 0LW

First published in 2002 by Hodder Wayland, an imprint of Hodder Children's Books

British Library Cataloguing in Publication Data
Harris, Nathaniel, 1937-
The Cuban missile crisis. – (History through newspapers)
1.Cuban Missile Crisis, 1962 – Sources – Juvenile
literature 2. Cuban Missile Crisis, 1962 – Press coverage –
Juvenile literature
I. Title
973.9'22

ISBN 075024182 9

Printed and bound in Italy by G. Canale

Designer: Ian Winton
Cover design: Claire Bond
Series editors: Jane Tyler and Kathryn Walker
Picture research: Rachel Tisdale

learn.co.uk is a trade mark of Guardian Education Interactive Limited
and is used under license

Hodder Children's Books would like to thank the following for the loan of their material:
Corbis: Cover, page 7 Bettmann/Corbis, 11 Bettmann/Corbis, 12-13 Bettmann/Corbis, 18-19 Bettmann/Corbis,
23, 24-25, 29; **Daily Mail/Associated Newspapers (supplied by
University of Kent):** page 21; **Hulton Getty:** pages 4, 9, 16-17, 27.

Hodder Children's Books would like to thank the following for permission to reproduce newspaper articles: **by
kind permission of Atlantic Syndication for Associated Newspapers:** page 6; **News International Newspapers
Limited:** page 10 *The Times* 24/8/62, 12 *Daily Herald* 25/8/62; © **The Daily Mirror:** page 18; Copyright in the
newspaper extracts on pages 8, 14, 20, 22, 24, 28 © **Learnthings Limited and Guardian Newspapers Limited;**
Morning Star: page 26; © **Reuters:** page 10; © **Telegraph Group Limited 1962:** page 16.

Hodder Children's Books
A division of Hodder Headline Limited
338 Euston Road
London NW1 3BH

CONTENTS

THE COLD WAR

ABOUT THIS BOOK

This book presents a series of extracts from British newspapers published at the time of the Cuban Missile Crisis. A range of sources is used so that different opinions are represented. Each article deals with an important aspect of the crisis. On the same double page you will find key background information and a separate 'Evaluation' panel which explains difficult points in the extract and suggests how to approach it as a piece of historical evidence. For example, it asks whether the statements in the extracts are reliable and unbiased.

As newspapers appear daily or weekly, they deal with issues and events as they happen. To make money, they must sell in large numbers – which means that their contents must please their regular readers. So newspaper articles provide evidence about readers' opinions and attitudes.

Furthermore, each newspaper generally tries to attract particular groups of readers. It wants to please them, but also tries to keep or win their support for its policies. So a newspaper also tells us something about the ideas and aims of its owners and editors.

The Cold War lasted for over 40 years, from the late 1940s to the early 1990s. During this time, large areas of the world were divided between two alliances – two groups of nations that were bitterly hostile to each other.

On one side, the United States (USA) led an alliance of mostly **democratic** states such as Britain, France, Italy and West Germany. They were often referred to, for short, as 'the West'. The rival alliance was headed by the **Soviet Union** or **USSR**, a vast country that no longer exists. At that time it included Russia and a number of East European and Central Asian states that are now independent. The Soviet Union and its allies were known as the **communist bloc** because they lived under a

Rivals for world power: Soviet leader Khrushchev and US President Kennedy meeting in Vienna in 1961.

political and social system – **communism** – very different from the West's. This was one of the main reasons for the hostility between the two alliances.

Why was their long struggle called the Cold War? Because the hostile moves and counter-moves of the two sides never ended in a 'hot' war – that is, an all-out shooting war between the USA and USSR. But at times war was very close. This was a terrifying prospect, because both sides had nuclear weapons, capable of mass destruction on a scale never seen before in human history. The Cuban Missile Crisis was the moment in the Cold War when such a horror seemed most likely to happen.

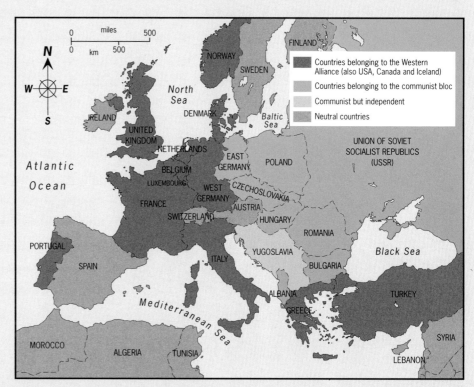

Divided Europe, as it was at the time of the 1962 Cuban Missile Crisis and remained, almost unchanged, until 1989.

Conflict of Ideas

The USA and most of its European allies were **democracies** in which people were free to choose their rulers. Most manufacturing and trading was carried out by independent private companies and individuals. This economic system is known as **capitalism**.

By contrast, the USSR and its allies were run by a single political party, the Communist Party, which allowed no opposition, and industry and businesses were owned and managed by the state. Despite its **dictatorial** features, communism had many supporters. They claimed that capitalist countries were really run by and for the rich, whereas communism shared out wealth among working people.

For both sides, newspapers and other **media** were important means to convince their own and other peoples that their cause was just. During the Cold War, almost all British papers supported the West and took an anti-Soviet line. But there were important differences between them, and these showed up in the course of the Cuban Missile Crisis.

FLASHPOINT CUBA

The number of **communist** countries had increased after World War II (1939-45), and the West thought of the **USSR** as **expansionist** and aggressive. So US army and nuclear bases were set up in many countries close to the USSR, intended to prevent possible Soviet invasions. But to the Soviets the bases seemed like launchpads for an attack on them.

During the Cold War, there were a number of flashpoints – places where conflict was most likely to occur and could lead to war. One was Berlin in Germany, which was divided between the Western and communist powers. Cuba also became a flashpoint. This happened in 1959, when a revolt in Cuba led by Fidel Castro overthrew the corrupt dictatorship of Fulgencio Batista.

EXERCISE WHAT?

Cuba riddle of US troop build-up

A massive build-up of American forces in the Caribbean this weekend started rumours throughout the United States of an impending invasion of Cuba.

The Defence Department officials insisted today, however, that the reinforcements are part of a military exercise due to take place off Puerto Rico this week.

About 20,000 men, 40 warships and carrier-based aircraft are taking part.

Pointers

The official denial did not stop at least one influential newspaper, the *Washington Post*, considered to have closer-than-most access to the **White House**, from carrying a front-page report hinting at a major development in the next 24 hours.

The newspaper pointed out as significant that President Kennedy had suddenly returned from Chicago to Washington, ostensibly [supposedly] suffering from a cold, although he attended Mass [Catholic religious service] this morning and was reported looking fit.

Vice-President Lyndon Johnson had unexpectedly returned from Honolulu, also said to be suffering from a cold.

Mr Dean Rusk, Secretary of State [foreign minister], had cancelled a trip to Hot Springs, Virginia.

Chiefs of Staff had been ordered not to leave Washington.

US Hostility

The US tended to suspect revolutionary governments like Castro's of being pro-communist, and Americans were angered when Castro introduced reforms, including a take-over of Cuba's sugar industry, which was largely US-owned. Castro may or may not have sympathized with **communism**, but hostile US policies, such as cutting off trade with Cuba, encouraged him to turn to the communist **bloc**.

There had already been many alarms before the *Daily Mail* published this article on 22 October 1962, which asks why US forces are mobilizing.

Victory for a revolution: Fidel Castro and followers enter Havana in triumph on 1 January 1959.

The US also armed and trained Cuban exiles who opposed Castro, and in April 1961 US ships landed them on the island at the Bay of Pigs. They believed that the Cuban people would help the anti-Castro forces overthrow him. But instead they supported him and the invasion was a humiliating failure. In 1961 Castro declared Cuba the first communist state in the Americas, only 90 miles from the US coast. This enraged the US, which had long dominated the region and found communism in its 'back yard' intolerable. So further attacks on Cuba seemed likely and the Cubans asked for Soviet military aid.

Evaluation

The *Daily Mail's* article is a good example of journalistic detective work. Military exercises are 'war games', more or less realistic manoeuvres, carried out to make sure a country's armed forces are ready for war. But they can also mask preparations for real military operations, and the *Mail* suggested that this was happening. It backed up its view by showing that US leaders were assembling at the centre of government, Washington, DC. The president's cold, it implied, was just an excuse for him to return to his headquarters.

There were many rumours and alarms during the Cold War. The exercises might or might not have been genuine. The *Mail's* suggestion turned out to be the right one, though no British newspaper yet knew the full story.

The text in square brackets here and in other newspaper articles in this book has been added to explain certain words, terms or references.

THE CRISIS BREAKS

On the evening of Monday 22 October, 1962, the president of the United States, John F Kennedy, told his nation on TV and radio that Soviet experts were constructing nuclear missile sites in Cuba, and that Soviet ships were currently delivering missiles to the island. These were offensive weapons – missiles that could be launched against the American mainland, not for use against an invader.

Kennedy and his advisers had kept the situation a secret for some time, until their suspicions were confirmed and they had decided what to do. Photographs taken over Cuba by a US spy-plane on 14 October had provided unmistakable evidence that missile sites were being built. After a week of discussions, Kennedy decided against an immediate invasion, or a bombing of the **installations**, in favour of a 'quarantine'.

US IMPOSES CUBAN ARMS BLOCKADE

Ready to sink Soviet ships if necessary

UN URGED TO ACT

The United States is prepared to sink Soviet ships if necessary to prevent offensive weapons reaching Cuba. This was stated by the Defence Department here tonight after President Kennedy had ordered an arms blockade of the island.

Mr Kennedy, announcing in a broadcast 'a strict quarantine' to stop an offensive **communist** build-up, including the sending of missiles, had said: 'All ships of any kind ... will, if found to contain cargoes of offensive weapons, be turned back.' But Cubans would not be denied the necessities of life.

Later a Defence Department spokesman said the United States had placed its forces, including its **garrison** in Berlin and the Strategic Air Command [the US military air force] on a world wide alert. Other officials said a showdown could come with the **Soviet Union** in 24 hours.

If a ship did not stop when ordered to do so, it was stated, a shot would be fired across its bows. If it still did not stop or turn back, then another shot would be fired at it with the idea of minimizing any casualties. The blockade, the formal proclamation of which was expected to be signed by the president tomorrow, would apply to ships of all nations, including Allied vessels.

The *Manchester Guardian* of 23 October 1962 breaks the news of the Cuban Missile Crisis.

The 'Quarantine'

This was really a **blockade**. The US navy would stop and search all ships headed for Cuba, and would not allow them to deliver arms. 'Quarantine' was a strange term to use, since it normally described the enforced isolation of a diseased person who might infect others. The president probably wanted to avoid the word 'blockade' because it was usually a wartime term with complicated legal implications.

Kennedy stated that the US would not prevent food and other necessities from reaching Cuba. At the same time US forces continued to **mobilize**, in preparation for a possible invasion. Clearly he was trying to be firm without appearing to look for a fight. Even so, a blockade posed a risk that Soviet ships would refuse to be searched, and that shots would be fired, leading to war.

Evaluation

The *Manchester Guardian* article was mainly a straightforward report on a piece of red-hot news, summarizing statements by Kennedy and the Defence Department. For the sake of impact, the report emphasized essential phrases and left out what it considered to be less important parts. Omitted passages were indicated by suspension dots [...].

Though generally pro-Western, the *Manchester Guardian* was not aggressively anti-communist and tended to favour peaceful, negotiated solutions to conflicts. Unlike many papers, the *Manchester Guardian* gave prominence to '**UN** urged to act' – UN being short for **United Nations**, the international organization that brought together most of the world's governments and was intended to help them resolve their differences.

The White House on TV: US president John F Kennedy announces to the world the 'quarantine' of Cuba on 24 October.

LOOMING CONFLICT

With a Soviet **flotilla** reported to be nearing Cuba, a US-Soviet clash began to seem inevitable. It would be hard for either side to give way. Whichever retreated would suffer a terrible blow to its prestige. The political careers of the US and Soviet leaders were also at stake.

The Soviet prime minister, Nikita Khrushchev, was a shrewd 68-year-old who had led the **USSR** since 1953. He believed that **communism** would triumph over all the world, but stated that this could happen peacefully. Though he wanted to avoid the horrors of a nuclear war, Khrushchev often lost his temper and behaved in rude and provoking ways.

The US president, John F Kennedy, was 45 – at that time unusually young for a national leader. Since he was also handsome, Kennedy was seen as a glamorous, film-star-like figure. He was actually a hard-headed politician, and Khrushchev may well have underestimated him.

25 RUSSIAN SHIPS MOVING TOWARDS CUBA

ARMED BOARDING PARTIES STAND READY

PRESIDENTIAL PROCLAMATION DEFINES BLOCKADE

Washington – Mr McNamara, US Secretary of Defence, said tonight that about 25 Soviet cargo ships were moving towards Cuba and armed boarding parties would be ready to search them when the US **blockade** went into effect tomorrow. – *Reuters*

FROM OUR OWN CORRESPONDENT
President Kennedy signed a proclamation tonight formally establishing an arms blockade of Cuba from 2 pm **GMT** tomorrow but stating that force would only be used if a vessel refused to comply with instructions.

The proclamation, entitled 'Interdiction [prohibition] of the delivery of offensive weapons to Cuba', authorized Mr McNamara, the Secretary of Defence, to use the land, sea, and air forces of the United States, and the forces of such Latin [Central and South] American countries as should be made available, to prevent the delivery of offensive weapons to Cuba. Offensive weapons were defined as surface-to-surface missiles and bombs; air-to-surface rockets and guided missiles; the **warheads** for any of the above missiles; the mechanical equipment required to operate the missiles, and any other classes of weapons to be designated by the Secretary of Defence at a later date.

On 24 October 1962, *The Times* headlines a threatened clash between US and Soviet ships.

Labels on photo:
MISSILE ERECTOR
CABLE
MISSILE SHELTER TENT
TRACKED PRIME MOVERS
OXIDIZER TANK TRAILERS
FUEL TANK TRAILERS

The evidence: one of many photos taken by US spy-planes over Cuba, showing Soviet missile launch sites.

Evaluation

The Times' headlines captured the drama of the situation, with the ships approaching and the US determined to intercept them. Like many Western newspapers, The Times used 'Russian' as though it meant Soviet (Russia was by far the largest state of the USSR). Reuters is a famous British news agency — an organization that gathers news from all over the world and distributes it to many papers. But newspapers are not completely dependent on agencies for information; if they were, they might be receiving wrong or biased reports. Papers also have their own reporters, or correspondents, stationed in important places such as Washington.

The focus of the article was US determination, and it went on to give the text of the president's proclamation and the backing he received from Latin American states — except, of course, Cuba.

A Soviet Gamble?

Kennedy also had one supreme advantage – the United States' overwhelming superiority in nuclear weapons. Though the fact was not made fully clear to their peoples, both Western and **communist** leaders knew this was so. But while the US could defeat the USSR in a nuclear war, even the winner would suffer and millions would die. So neither side wanted an all-out war, though they were sometimes prepared to risk one. In these circumstances, putting missiles on Cuba has often been seen as a reckless gamble by Khrushchev.

SOVIET MOTIVES

Khrushchev had several motives for establishing bases on Cuba. One was a genuine wish to protect the island. The failure of the US-backed Bay of Pigs invasion had infuriated Kennedy, who ordered secret operations to ruin the Cuban economy and assassinate Fidel Castro. Another invasion seemed likely. Soviet missiles on Cuba would surely make the Americans hesitate before attacking again.

They would also improve the **USSR's** military position. The US was already much the stronger, had ringed the **Soviet Union** with bases, and was now developing new weapons. Soviet missiles, capable of hitting the American homeland within a few minutes of launch, would go some way to evening things up. Khrushchev also resented the missiles recently installed by the US in Turkey, close to the Soviet frontier. These were 'offensive' – capable of wiping out Soviet cities – and placing missiles in Cuba was a form of tit-for-tat.

THE REAL CHALLENGE

President Kennedy's evidence has been published. It has convinced the British government – and will convince most of the world – that the Russians ARE building missile bases in Cuba. The president is blockading Cuba in order to get rid of these bases. His reasons are understandable, although the *Herald* does not accept them as conclusive.

It is no use mincing words. The **blockade** is an act of force by America against Cuba, an independent country with which America is not at war.

If Mr Kruschev were to choose to answer force with force, the world might be on the verge of nuclear conflict.

The contradiction
The **communist** bases in Cuba are provocative. And the Russians lied about them. But they are only part of a world problem.

America has bases, too, surrounding the Soviet Union. If the American nuclear bases are defensive, then Cuba's Fidel Castro can claim that so are his.

That point was underlined by Walter Lippmann, the most famous of American political commentators, in his important article printed in the *Herald* yesterday.

As Mr Lippmann said, America can no longer encircle the Soviet [Union] with military bases AND insist there must be no communist base anywhere on the American continent.

(Left) A *Daily Herald* **article of 25 October 1962 gives the newspaper's verdict on some Cuban issues.**

For and Against

Most Western governments and **media** supported the US, seeing the Soviet missiles as part of a communist plan for world domination. They emphasized the fact that the missiles had been installed secretly and that the Soviets refused to admit what they had done even after the spy-plane photographs were published. Newspapers generally argued that the US had to act decisively.

Evaluation

This type of article is known as an editorial or leader. It is not a piece of factual reporting but offers the newspaper's comments and opinions.

The *Herald's* editorial skilfully mixed pro- and anti-American points to show it was unbiased. It condemned Khrushchev's action as 'provocative', but pointed out that the US had no right in international law to interfere with ships in peacetime.

Note that the *Daily Herald* has a different version of Khrushchev's name — one of several to be found in Western newspapers. Various versions were possible because the Russian alphabet is different from that used in the West. But the inaccuracy of Western versions of 'Khrushchev' shows a strangely careless attitude — not shared by Western communists (page 26).

However, there were also papers that tried to take a more balanced view. The *Daily Herald* was one of several that recognized the illegality of the American blockade and the Soviet Union's right to supply its ally with arms. The paper hinted at a possible trade-off between US and Soviet bases, an idea that would eventually play a part in ending the crisis.

April 1961: captured Cuban exiles are marched away after the failure of the US-backed Bay of Pigs invasion in 1961.

13

AVOIDING A SHOWDOWN

The news that some Soviet ships were turning away from Cuba was received with relief. The Soviet action could have been seen as a surrender, but Khrushchev seized the opportunity to present himself as a man of peace. He took this line in answering a letter from Bertrand Russell, a famous philosopher who led campaigns in favour of **nuclear disarmament**. Khrushchev promised that the **USSR** would do nothing rash, despite US 'aggression', and said that he was ready for direct talks with Kennedy.

The United Nations

When there were conflicts between states, the **United Nations** (**UN**) usually became involved in efforts to make peace. But as an organization the UN had no power of its own. Its most important official, the Secretary-General, tried to end conflicts by meeting national leaders and suggesting truces or compromise solutions.

In 1962 U Thant, a Burmese, was acting Secretary-General. He contacted Khrushchev and Kennedy, proposing that the Soviets should stop shipping arms to Cuba while the US suspended its naval **blockade**. Despite Khrushchev's letter to Russell, there was no certainty that either side would agree to U Thant's proposals.

SOME SOVIET SHIPS ALTER COURSE

Mr K ready for Summit talks on Cuba

APPEAL BY U THANT

The American Defence Department last night confirmed that some of the 25 ships of the Soviet **block** bound for Cuba had altered course. Other vessels were continuing towards the island, 'but no intervention has yet been necessary.'

This was one of several more hopeful signs. Earlier the Tass agency quoted a letter on Cuba sent by the Soviet premier in reply to a telegram by Bertrand Russell, in which Mr Khrushchev said 'We would regard it as useful to have a Summit meeting.'

While promising to 'take no rash decisions,' he gave this warning: 'As long as rocket-nuclear weapons have not been used there is a possibility of averting war. Once the Americans have launched aggression, a Summit meeting will become impossible and useless.' Mr Khrushchev also sent a letter to Mr Kennedy, but making no mention of a Summit.

Meanwhile new initiatives were being taken at the United Nations. U Thant, the acting Secretary-General, sent letters appealing to Mr Khrushchev to suspend arms shipments to Cuba and to President Kennedy to suspend the blockade. Both suspensions would be for two to three weeks.

The *Manchester Guardian* of 25 October 1962 reports on the latest developments in the crisis.

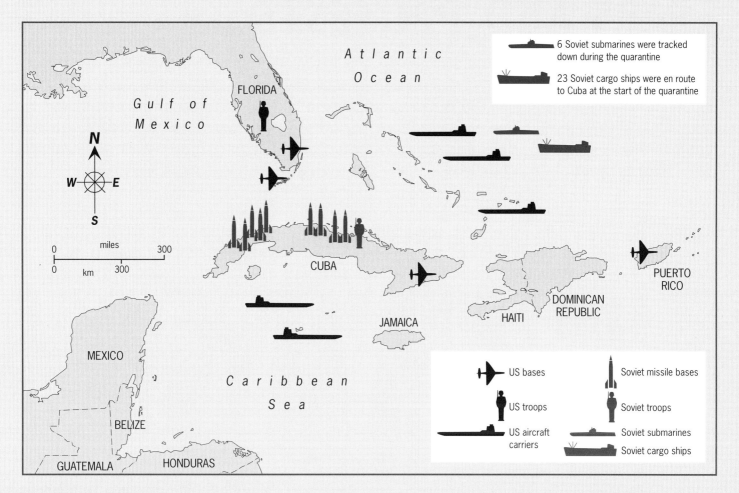

Key:

6 Soviet submarines were tracked down during the quarantine

23 Soviet cargo ships were en route to Cuba at the start of the quarantine

✈ US bases

👤 US troops

🚢 US aircraft carriers

🚀 Soviet missile bases

👤 Soviet troops

🚢 Soviet submarines

🚢 Soviet cargo ships

October 1962: US and Soviet forces, face to face in the Caribbean. Note how close Cuba is to the US mainland.

Evaluation

In this main piece, the *Manchester Guardian* picked out several key events that gave reason for optimism and squeezed them into its main front-page report. It gave the US Defence Department's news of the altered course of some Soviet ships. It quoted the official Soviet news agency, Tass, about Khrushchev's willingness to attend a Summit (a meeting of heads of governments, in this instance Kennedy and Khrushchev). And it noted the efforts of the UN Secretary-General, U Thant, to calm down the situation.

This issue of the *Manchester Guardian* carried so many articles about the Cuban Missile Crisis that an index to them was provided on the front page. The paper obviously thought that readers would want to know about every aspect of such a frightening crisis. In the main story, the emphasis on positive developments showed how much people feared a nuclear war and welcomed hopeful news.

FEARS AND PROTESTS

In 1962 there were so many nuclear weapons in the world that it was being said a great war would destroy civilization. Even an accident or misunderstanding might cause a catastrophe. This situation led to the development of movements to promote peace. Britain possessed nuclear weapons of its own, and two organizations (the Campaign for **Nuclear Disarmament** or CND and the Committee of 100) campaigned strongly against them. They argued that Britain should take the lead and give up these weapons.

These organizations did not necessarily represent the majority of the British people, but they were very active, and the Cuban Missile Crisis stirred them to make new efforts.

Sixth Formers 'Strike' over Cuba Blockade

Town parade, then 40 send petition to premier

Forty sixth formers at the co-educational grammar school at Midhurst, Sussex, went on 'strike' yesterday as a protest against President Kennedy's Cuba **blockade** and what they called 'the degenerating world situation.'

They refused to attend classes, although they were willing to continue prefects' duties and private study. The strikers, 34 boys and six girls, also took part in a two-mile protest march through the town, carrying posters on hockey sticks with such slogans as 'The next war will be the last.' Wearing their school blazers, they halted outside the parish church, where they encircled the war memorial and stood in silence. Then they returned to the school to send a petition to Mr Macmillan.

It read: 'We deplore the way in which the world situation is being allowed to degenerate into one in which war is imminent, and demand that the government takes every possible step to end this state of affairs.

'Therefore, in order to impress upon the British public our convictions in this matter, we are not participating in any lessons.'

The *Daily Telegraph* of 25 October 1962 describes a protest against war.

Evaluation

The *Daily Telegraph* article described an event – a school strike – that was unusual and therefore newsworthy. Also unusual in 1962 was the idea of sixth-formers sending a petition to the British prime minister, Mr Macmillan. There are inverted commas around 'strike' because it was not a strike in the normal sense – of paid employees refusing to work.

'Strike' may also have been intended to suggest that it should not be taken too seriously. Perhaps because it disapproved of protest movements, the *Telegraph* focused on a local event that many readers may have thought amusing, giving it more space than the marches that were taking place in London and other British cities.

Around the World

The crisis also involved people who were not normally protesters. Some people were moved by the threat of war, others by anger at what they saw as the bullying of a small country (Cuba) by a great power (the USA). Marchers in Manchester carried placards saying 'Hands off Cuba!' and there were protests and signs of alarm in many other countries. In Switzerland, people rushed to stock up on food, while Americans bought **fall-out shelters** that might protect them from radiation after a nuclear war. In the **communist** countries, protests against government policies were not allowed, but even so, there were signs that Soviet citizens were deeply worried and wanted peace above all.

No war over Cuba! In London, marchers belonging to CND (Campaign for Nuclear Disarmament) stage a sit-down.

SPARRING AT THE UN

On Thursday 26 October, Khrushchev and Kennedy replied to U Thant's proposals for a truce. This appeared to show that both leaders were serious about finding a peaceful solution to the crisis. But there was no real progress, since the US refused to make **concessions** while the Soviets went on constructing missile bases for weapons they had already shipped to Cuba.

However, Kennedy was determined to minimize the possibility of a conflict. When a Soviet oil tanker approached Cuba, it was stopped by a US naval patrol. But after the Soviet captain declared that the vessel carried only petroleum, the patrol allowed it to go on without being searched. The US knew that the tanker had set off before the crisis had begun, and so was unlikely to be carrying hidden weaponry when other Soviet ships – presumably those carrying arms – had turned back.

UN War of Words

Khrushchev's speedy and favourable reply to U Thant made a good impression. But the US hit back in the propaganda battle. The Soviets had still not admitted that their **installations** on Cuba were surface-to-surface missiles, capable of hitting the American mainland. This led to an angry encounter at the Security Council, a **UN** body on which representatives of the most powerful countries sat. The US Ambassador to the UN, Adlai Stevenson, showed the spy-plane photographs.

The *Daily Mirror* of 26 October 1962 reports on negotiations at the UN.

Scrap Cuba bases first, says Kennedy

TRUCE OFFER BY K – BUT BLOCKADE IS TO STAY

Russia's Premier Krushchev and America's President Kennedy tonight replied to the appeal of **United Nations'** chief U Thant for a two to three weeks' 'truce' in the Cuban crisis.

Krushchev agreed to suspend arms shipments during the 'truce' – if Kennedy lifted his naval **blockade**.

But he was silent on the vital point in U Thant's peace call last night – that work on Soviet missile bases in Cuba should stop.

Kennedy said the Cuban missile bases must be scrapped. America was willing to hold preliminary truce talks.

He said nothing about his blockade. But later, the **White House** said it would continue – because Soviet ships were still heading towards Castro's island.

Krushchev beat Kennedy to the **propaganda** gun. The Soviet reply was announced about half an hour before the United Nations Security Council – at which Kennedy's reply was to be read – resumed its Cuban debate.

WEAPONS

Krushchev said U Thant's proposal was 'in the interests of peace'.

Kennedy assured U Thant of his 'desire to reach a satisfactory and peaceful solution.'

He made his 'Scrap the rockets!' call in these words: 'The existing threat was created by the secret introduction of offensive weapons into Cuba, and the answer lies in the removal of such weapons.'

18

The American case: aerial photographs taken by US spy-planes are shown at the Security Council of the UN. The US ambassador, Adlai Stevenson (far right at circular table), and the Soviet ambassador, Valerian Zorin (far left at circular table), are present – and about to argue violently.

Then he demanded that the Soviet Ambassador, Valerian Zorin, should answer Yes or No – did the **USSR** have missile bases on Cuba? Zorin answered that he wouldn't reply on demand, like a criminal in court. Perhaps he had a point, but this refusal strengthened the impression that the Soviets had been lying all along.

Evaluation

The *Daily Mirror's* front page article looks like a straightforward report of events. But it actually mixed in the newspaper's comments with the facts. The *Mirror* strongly supported Kennedy, which may be why it pounced on the hole in Khrushchev's apparently enthusiastic acceptance of U Thant's message — its silence on the question of removing the missiles and bases.

The paper also identified the propaganda element in Khrushchev's timing of his reply to U Thant. By contrast, President Kennedy's statements were just recorded or quoted — which, it could be argued, gave the impression that his words were honest expressions of his views or even the simple truth about the situation.

RISING TENSION

After two days when there were some signs of hope, alarming headlines appeared again on Saturday 27 October. The Soviet decision to pull back their ships had avoided a clash over the **blockade** and bought time for negotiations. But now another urgent issue had emerged. The **USSR** already had a substantial number of technicians in Cuba, as well as missiles and the equipment with which to build bases. US information was that the Soviets were hurrying to make the bases operational – that is, ready for action.

Kennedy believed he must do something about the bases before their rockets were trained on American cities. This meant that he would have to act very soon; and the only alternatives seemed to be to bomb the bases or invade Cuba.

US THREATENS NEW MOVE AGAINST CUBA

Missile build-up goes ahead 'rapidly'

EFFORT AT CAMOUFLAGE

The United States, after drawing attention to the possibility of 'further action' against Cuba if the offensive military preparations there continued, announced last night that the build-up of missile sites in the island was going ahead rapidly, with efforts to camouflage them.

The announcement said this activity 'apparently is directed at achieving a full operational capability as soon as possible.' It was issued when speculation was growing in Washington on the prospects that Americans might seek to destroy the missile sites by 'pin-point' bombing or even invasion.

While this grave new possibility was developing, the immediate danger of armed clash between US and Soviet ships in the Caribbean was being averted, as the result of consultations and new direct appeals by Acting **UN** Secretary-General U Thant, to the two sides. Mr Kennedy told him the US would agree to his request that 'our vessels in the Caribbean will do everything possible to avoid a confrontation,' and Mr Khrushchev promised that Soviet ships would be diverted from the interception area [the area patrolled by the American navy].

Agonizing Decisions

All through the crisis, Kennedy's public statements sounded tough and uncompromising. But records of meetings and eye-witness statements – made public only years later – show that he was nervous and deeply troubled. He knew that a miscalculation on his part could cause the deaths of millions of people, but he felt unable to allow the Soviet build-up to continue. So he ordered further **mobilizations** of US forces and detailed planning for an invasion of Cuba.

A *Manchester Guardian* article of 27 October 1962 describes the American reaction to work on the Soviet missile sites on Cuba.

Evaluation

The *Manchester Guardian's* front-page article emphasized the seriousness of the crisis, quoting a US government announcement made on the previous (Friday) night. Its tone of alarm was reinforced by other features on the same page, including one headed 'Talk of a nuclear attack'.

In the headline, the inverted commas (quote marks) around 'rapidly' were intended to show that the word was not the *Manchester Guardian's* but had been used by some other source — in this instance, the US government. 'Pin-point' bombing means bombing so accurate that it can destroy a target without hurting outsiders. Claims of pin-point accuracy have generally been made to convince the public that there would be few civilian casualties — an important matter where a powerful state such as the USA takes military action against a country with which it is not officially at war.

Eyeball to eyeball, hands locked and fingers over the button: a *Daily Mail* cartoonist's view of the crisis. Despite the humour of cartoons such as this, many people were deeply afraid that the crisis would end in nuclear war.

A WAY OUT?

By the time the *Observer* appeared on the morning of Sunday 28 October, the world had come very close to war. Much, but not all, of the behind-the-scenes drama became known to the media very quickly. There had been a new development on Friday night, too late for Saturday morning newspapers like the *Manchester Guardian* to receive news of it. Mr Khrushchev had sent a personal letter to Kennedy proposing a deal. He claimed that the Soviet weapons were in Cuba only because the US was threatening to overthrow Castro's government: if Kennedy would promise not to invade Cuba, the **USSR** would withdraw its missiles. Khrushchev obviously took the situation very seriously, appealing to Kennedy to stay calm and not risk plunging the world into war.

Khrushchev's letter was welcome, and for a moment it seemed that the crisis was over. But the next morning another, more official-sounding message arrived from the Soviet government.

Khrushchev offers Turkey bases swap

KENNEDY: NO DEAL TILL CUBA MISSILES ARE MADE USELESS

Then settlement 'in two days'

President Kennedy again stated his terms late tonight for a peaceful settlement of the Cuban crisis. He told Mr Khrushchev a settlement could be reached in two days; but first the bases in Cuba must be rendered inoperable [unusable].

In a letter the president wrote that he is willing to remove his **blockade** of Cuba and talk about a 'permanent solution to the Cuba problem' along lines suggested by Mr Khrushchev. But he will not talk until work has ceased on missile bases in Cuba and until all weapons systems there have been made inoperable 'under effective **United Nations** arrangements.'

The letter was handed to the Soviet **Embassy** at 9. It was his answer to the first of two letters he has had from the Russian leader. Earlier in the day a **White House** statement taunted the Russians with having made 'several inconsistent and conflicting proposals within the last 24 hours.'

The contents of the first Khrushchev letter have not been revealed but a White House source said that it did not refer to Turkey. The second letter, which became known first through a Tass dispatch from Moscow this morning, suggested a swap whereby America would pull **NATO** [US-led alliance] bases out of Turkey if the Russians would pull their bases out of Cuba. The president made it known that he had rejected the swap shortly after noon Washington time today.

The *Observer* of 28 October describes the exchanges between Khrushchev and Kennedy

On the Brink

The new message proposed the same deal, but added that the US must also agree to withdraw its missiles from Turkey. The Soviets' intentions had again become unclear. Other incidents increased the tension in the White House. After the shooting down of a spy-plane over Cuba, US military men demanded a strike back, but Kennedy put off action for one more day.

The president's brother and close adviser, Robert Kennedy, convinced him that there was a way of responding positively to the Soviet messages. In his reply, the president simply ignored the second message and agreed to the terms proposed in the first. But how would Khrushchev react?

Family conference: Kennedy and his brother Robert (left), the US Attorney General. Robert Kennedy was very influential during the Cuban crisis.

Evaluation

Like other Western newspapers, the *Observer* offered a great deal of up-to-date information on the crisis. One of the things that made this possible was the fact that Kennedy made public many of his exchanges with Khrushchev.

This made Kennedy seem firm and open — though of course there were secret talks and arrangements that the **media** knew nothing about. It also ensured that newspapers headlined the US view of the situation. Here, the *Observer* implied that Kennedy was restating his terms and taking a tough line; this received more emphasis than his agreement to a solution to the Cuban problem along the lines suggested by Khrushchev.

AGREEMENT REACHED

On Monday 29 October, newspaper headlines proclaimed the good news: Khrushchev had agreed to withdraw the Soviet missiles from Cuba in return for a US guarantee that it would not invade the island. In the West, the agreement was generally seen as a triumph for Kennedy, but the president made a point of not trying to humiliate Khrushchev, calling the Soviet leader's action 'statesmanlike'.

Kennedy had good reason for not humiliating Khrushchev. In Moscow, as in Washington, there were people among the leaders who favoured taking a tougher line and even going to war. Clearly Kennedy did not want Khrushchev to be regarded as a failure and replaced as leader by someone less willing to compromise.

MR K AGREES TO AMERICAN DEMAND

The *Manchester Guardian* of 29 October 1962 announces the US-Soviet agreement.

Mr Khrushchev, in his letter to President Kennedy yesterday, announced that the Soviet Government had ordered the dismantling of offensive weapons in Cuba, their crating and return to the **Soviet Union**, 'to liquidate with greater speed the dangerous conflict' and 'to serve the cause of peace.'

In his letter he made no reference to his earlier suggestion, that the US should abandon its bases in Turkey. He pointed out, however, that the Soviet Union would not be indifferent to attempts to 'engender [create] uncertainty in the Cuban people... or to hinder them to build their new life undisturbed.'

Russia, said Mr Khrushchev, was ready to come to an agreement that **United Nations** representatives may verify that no offensive weapons are left in Cuba. He announced that he had sent Mr Kuznetsov, the first Deputy Foreign Minister, to New York to assist U Thant in his efforts to resolve the crisis.

(*Right*) Going home: a Soviet freighter (top of picture) leaves Cuba, the dismantled missiles clearly visible on its deck, accompanied by a US navy vessel.

A Secret Deal

There was also another reason. On the president's instructions, Robert Kennedy had approached the Soviet **ambassador** to the United States with a further offer. If Khrushchev accepted Kennedy's public offer of a guarantee in return for a Soviet withdrawal, the president promised that US missiles in Turkey would be quietly removed soon afterwards.

So Kennedy did in fact agree to the proposals in Khrushchev's letters, but only in secret. As this incident shows, newspapers are excellent sources for public history, but some things happen behind the scenes that only become known many years later.

Evaluation

This *Manchester Guardian* item summarized the Russian premier's letter fairly, but its headline told readers to think of it as a surrender to a US demand. Moreover it was not the main article — despite the fact that Khrushchev's letter was what actually ended the crisis. The main article and biggest headline focused on Kennedy's statements. Also given greater prominence was an article headlined 'Cold-war balance tilts towards the West', which again treated the agreement as a great US victory.

The *Manchester Guardian* noted that Khrushchev made no reference to his earlier proposal that the US should scrap its Turkish missile bases. It assumed — understandably but wrongly — that the **USSR** had given way on the issue.

SIGHS OF RELIEF

Fearful people all round the world sighed with relief at the news of a US-Soviet deal. Congratulations flowed into the **White House**, for Kennedy was widely felt to have emerged victorious from a showdown with Khrushchev.

The situation in the **USSR** was harder to assess, because the **media** and Soviet citizens were closely controlled. But there were signs that ordinary people, like those in the West, were relieved that the threat of a world war had been lifted.

Against the Deal

Not everyone was pleased. Some of the leading US military men felt that Kennedy had been weak in agreeing not to attack Cuba, and there was an angry meeting between the president and General Curtis Le May. Kennedy had also promised the many Cuban exiles in the US that Castro would be overthrown, and they too felt angry and betrayed. The pressures on Khrushchev are less clear. There were signs that having to withdraw the missiles weakened his prestige within the ruling group, but he certainly remained in charge. After his fall from power in 1964, he praised Kennedy's moderation but still insisted that 'It was a great victory for us...that we had been able to extract from Kennedy a promise that neither America nor her allies would invade Cuba.'

STRENGTHEN THE PRESSURE

The whole world welcomes Mr Khrushchov's efforts to pull mankind back from the abyss of the nuclear war to which it was brought by the American **blockade** and threat to invade Cuba. His willingness to withdraw the weapons to which President Kennedy takes exception [objects], provided the US guarantees there will be no invasion, proves that these weapons were there to defend Cuba and not to attack America.

The threat of invasion was not new. Last year President Kennedy approved an attempted invasion of Cuban **counter-revolutionaries** [opponents of Castro's revolution] who had been trained in America and equipped with American weapons.

That attack was beaten off. But the nuclear wild men in the US campaigned with greater ferocity than ever for the overthrow by force of the Cuban government, demanding the fullest strength of American armed force should be openly used.

Don't relax

It was this threat which brought the Soviet weapons to Cuba. If that threat is removed, those weapons become unnecessary, and can also be removed, says Mr Khrushchov.

And so we breathe again.

A *Daily Worker* editorial gives the **communist** view of the situation on 29 October.

Castro, with Khrushchev, is greeted warmly on his visit to Moscow in May 1963. The alliance between Cuba and the USSR, though shaken by the missile crisis, continued.

Evaluation

The *Daily Worker* was the newspaper of the British Communist Party, and normally supported Soviet policies. Notice that its version of Khrushchev's name is the most accurate one (though not generally used even now).

The *Worker's* editorial naturally interpreted Khrushchev's action in the most favourable way. In its view, the Soviet missiles were installed solely to meet a US threat. To emphasize the reality of the threat, it reminded readers of the earlier US-backed invasion. Once the threat was removed, the missiles could go – 'proving' that they had only ever been in Cuba for defensive purposes. The *Worker* simply ignored the alternative explanation – that Khrushchev had had wider plans but had backed down.

THE AFTERMATH

The agreement between Kennedy and Khrushchev ended the crisis, although disputes continued for months over **UN** inspections and other matters. The Soviet weapons were removed, and in the early months of 1963 the US took its missiles out of Turkey.

Both the Americans and the Soviets realized that, during the crisis, peace had been threatened by slow communications. As a result, a 'hot line' was installed – a direct telephonic link between the American and Soviet leaders. In November 1963, Kennedy was assassinated in Dallas, Texas. Khrushchev was forced into retirement in 1964.

THE BURDEN ON MR KENNEDY

President Kennedy has won admiration for his handling of the Cuban crisis – both for the decisive action he took and for his readiness to be conciliatory at the end. Warm praise came for him from Mr Macmillan [the prime minister] and Mr Gaitskell [the Labour Party leader]. By resourcefulness and courage he has forced the Russians to retreat for the first time in 16 years, but he has not gloated over Mr Khrushchev. He has left the way open for renewed discussion on disarmament, Berlin and even on Cuba. May the opportunities be taken.

Looking at the crisis in retrospect [knowing how it turned out], one must acknowledge, the **blockade** and the American **mobilization** brought results far more beneficial than seemed probable a week ago. Events have justified Mr Kennedy's toughness. But, while fully recognizing that, one may also mention some less comforting aspects. First, the principle that might is right has gained precedence over the principle that disputes should be settled by peaceful means. The pledges in the **United Nations** Charter have been broken. A blockade was imposed in peacetime, armed aircraft were sent over another nation's territory, and a massive military invasion of that territory was threatened. Had this been done by any other country, the Americans themselves would have called it aggression. It was aggression; even if it was also rough justice.

Just after the end of the crisis, on 31 October 1962, the *Manchester Guardian* sums up.

News and Secrets

The Cold War went on under new leaders. But although there were revolutions and wars in various parts of the world, there was no military conflict between the superpowers – the USA and the **USSR**. Eventually, in 1989-91, the economic and military strain proved too much for most of the **communist** states. In Eastern Europe, and then in the **Soviet Union** itself, **communism** collapsed and the Cold War ended.

During the period, newspapers sometimes held back from publishing information that might endanger the country. But many Cold War facts were unknown to the **media**. Kennedy's willingness to remove US missiles from Turkey was kept secret. And in 1987 it was revealed that he would have gone even further for the sake of peace by publicly agreeing to withdraw. Khrushchev never guessed this, and Kennedy emerged from the crisis with the tough reputation described in the *Manchester Guardian*.

Evaluation

This *Manchester Guardian* editorial is a thoughtful piece. During the crisis the paper had doubts about the wisdom of US policy. But in this issue, which appeared days after its end, the *Manchester Guardian* admitted that 'Events have justified Mr Kennedy's toughness.'

However, the editorial regretted that the victory had been won by force — by an illegal blockade and an aggressive stance. The Soviets had (in the *Manchester Guardian's* view) provoked the crisis, which is why the outcome was 'rough justice'. But it was still aggression. The *Manchester Guardian* would have preferred a world in which disputes were settled by peaceful negotiations, with the United Nations playing a key role — a hope that had not been realized even at the beginning of the 21st century.

Murder in Dallas, Texas. Just one year after the missile crisis, Kennedy slumps in the back of his car after being shot on 22 November 1963.

TIMELINE

14 March 1953 — Nikita Sergeyevich Khrushchev becomes first secretary of the Soviet Communist Party and the most powerful figure in the USSR. In 1958 be becomes prime minister as well.

1 January 1959 — Fidel Castro's victorious revolutionary army enters Havana, capital of Cuba. Castro will become Cuban president.

3 January 1961 — The USA breaks off diplomatic relations with Cuba.

20 January 1961 — John F Kennedy is sworn in as 35th president of the USA. He is the youngest man to hold the office.

19 April 1961 — Cuban exiles land at the Bay of Pigs in Cuba. The US-backed invasion is a complete failure.

1 May 1961 — Castro proclaims Cuba a communist state.

14 October 1962 — A US spy-plane takes photographs indicating that there are Soviet missile bases in Cuba.

22 October 1962 — In a broadcast, Kennedy reveals the presence of the missile bases and announces a naval 'quarantine' (blockade) of Cuba.

23 October 1962 — Khrushchev denounces the US action. Soviet cargo ships continue on course for Cuba.

24 October 1962 — The quarantine begins. Some of the Soviet ships turn back. U Thant of the United Nations appeals to both sides. There are marches for peace in a number of countries, and in some places fights break out between pro- and anti-American demonstrators.

26 October 1962 — Kennedy and Khrushchev reply to U Thant. The US announces that the Soviets are trying to make their missile sites operational as quickly as possible. The US threatens further action.

27 October 1962 — Morning: Kennedy receives a message sent by Khrushchev the night before. Then a second and different message arrives with a fresh demand. The Americans are angered by the shooting down of a US spy-plane over Cuba. Many US advisers press for an invasion of the island, but Kennedy sends a public message to Khrushchev and also makes a secret promise about US bases in Turkey.

28 October 1962 — Khrushchev agrees to Kennedy's proposals. The crisis is over.

GLOSSARY

AMBASSADOR: High-ranking representative of a country, attached to a foreign state or the United Nations.

BLOC, or sometimes **BLOCK:** Group of closely allied states.

BLOCKADE: Naval action that prevents ships from entering a foreign port or ports.

CAPITALISM: Economic system based on the private ownership and running of industries and businesses.

COMMUNISM: Political and economic system based on rule by the Communist Party, and public or state ownership and running of industries and businesses (adjective and noun: **communist**).

CONCESSION: Something yielded to an opponent during an argument or negotiation. Concessions may be made by one or both sides for the sake of reaching an argreement.

COUNTER-REVOLUTIONARIES: People who wish to overthrow a revolutionary government and go back to the previous political system.

DEMOCRACY: Political system in which the people choose their own government through fair and free elections (adjective: **democratic**).

DICTATORSHIP: Rule by an individual or group which permits no opposition (adjective: **dictatorial**).

EMBASSY: Residence and offices of an AMBASSADOR and his staff.

EXPANSIONIST: Describes a state that wishes to increase the territory it controls.

FALL-OUT SHELTERS: Shelters designed to protect people during a nuclear war – not from the direct effects of explosions, but from the poisonous radioactive material ('fall-out') left in the air afterwards.

FLOTILLA: A large group of ships.

GARRISON: The troops defending a fort, town or other relatively small place.

GMT: Greenwich Mean Time: the time according to clocks in Britain, as opposed to the time in places further west or east, in different time zones.

INSTALLATION: Putting something into place. Also describes something that has been put into place.

MEDIA: General word for newspapers, TV, films, radio and other forms of mass communication.

MOBILIZATION: Calling people into the armed forces and assembling troops etc. in readiness to fight (verb: **mobilize**).

NATO: The North Atlantic Treaty organization. Military alliance led by the USA and mainly directed against the communist bloc.

NUCLEAR DISARMAMENT: Getting rid of nuclear weapons.

PROPAGANDA: Statements, usually distorted or even untrue, made to influence people's opinions on political or religious issues.

SOVIET UNION or USSR: Communist state which consisted of Russia, Ukraine, Belarus and other nations that are now independent. Also often referred to as 'the Soviets'.

UNITED NATIONS (UN): Organization, founded in 1945, to which most nations belong. Their representatives meet at the UN to try to solve international problems. UN officials play an independent role in disputes, and member-states supply troops for UN 'peace-keeping' operations.

USSR: see SOVIET UNION

WARHEAD: On rockets, the explosive device added to the main body.

WHITE HOUSE: Building in Washington, DC, where the US president lives. 'The White House' is often used to mean 'the US government' (compare 'Downing Street' for 'British government').

RESOURCES

Books

Harris, N, *Democracy*, 2001, Hodder Wayland

Richie, N, *Communism*, 2000, Hodder Wayland

Fowke, B, *The Cold War*, 2001, Hodder

Ross, S, *Causes of the Cold War*, 2001, Hodder Wayland

Taylor, D, *The Cold War*, 2001, Heinemann

Gibbs, T, *Fidel Castro: Leader of Cuba's revolution*, 2000, Hodder

Brogan, H, *Kennedy*, 1996, Longman

Downing, D, *John F Kennedy*, 2001, Heinemann

Campling, E, *The USSR since 1945*, 1990, Batsford

Fleming, F, *The Cuban Missile Crisis: to the brink of World War III*, 2001, Heinemann

Chrisp, P, *The Cuban Missile Crisis*, 2001, Hodder Wayland

Video cassettes

1962: A Year to Remember, Parkfield Pathe

Days That Shook the World, *volume 2: 1950-1979*, BBC

People's Century, *volume 7: 1959-1968*, BBC

Websites

The Cold War: www.cnn.com/SPECIALS/cold.war

Memories of Cuban Missile Crisis: www.stg.brown.edu

George Washington University – Cuban Missile Crisis: the Hidden History: www.gwu.edu Cuba Exhibit - Operation Mongoose/Plots to kill Castro: ------- www.jfk.org/Research/Cuba/Mongoose_Plots.htm

Visit www.learn.co.uk, the award-winning educational website backed by the *Guardian*, for exciting historical resources and online events.

INDEX